Seasons Change

Russella Lucien

Presentation by *BookLeaf Publishing*

Web: www.bookleafpub.com

E-mail: info@bookleafpub.com

ISBN: 9789357617659

First edition 2022

I dedicate this collection of poems to my family and friends. They provide endless amounts of support for my ideas and dreams.

Lake

1

Walking by the lake,
 sky turning red and orange,
sun sleeps in water

purple petals

Lilacs in sunlight,
Fragrant perfume surrounds me,
The smell of springtime

Apple picking

Heavy tree branches,
Fuji and Red Delicious ,
Unite for dessert

Autumn scene

Cool air and crisp breath,
Maple leaves fly through the sky,
I walk into fall

Tropical Walk

Fallen Palm leaves carpet the ground,
Pink hibiscus' frame the forest,
Humming birds flutter and drink the sweet
nectar from the flowers,
I feel the warm breath of humidity on the back
of my neck

The hum of crickets and bugs echo in the path,
A small lizard crosses in front of me,
The Gecko's green skin melting into the palm
leaves,
The faint aroma of Lilies fills my nose,

A Soft breeze kisses my shoulders,
Cerulean sky frames my head,
The house in the distance calls me,
I walk towards the curtains floating in the air

Thanksgiving

Gather around the table,
Set out the table cloth,
Platters of sliced turkey and roast beef,
Hash brown casserole sits beside stewed fish,
Lasagna sits beside bowls of rice,

Holding hands,
Giving thanks for the year,
Giving thanks to the creator,
Giving thanks for each other,

Apple Pie with nutmeg and cinnamon waft into
the air,
Wasail punch and hot tea sipped from tiny cups,
laughter and smiles all around,
This is Thanksgiving

Leaves

Orange, red, yellow and brown leaves,
painted in the sky,

Whoosh! Leaves flying in the cool crisp air,
Landing on the ground,
the bedding for making angels,

Let me hide in the leaves,
Let me cocoon in the colours,

Leaves blow in the breeze,
Let me catch them before the season ends,
Let me catch them before the air turns from cool
to cold.

Rain

Grey clouds wrinkled-up like a crumpled paper,
Grumble, grumble echoes in the air,
The sword of light striking the ground,
Creating sparks of electricity.

Pin drops of water hit my hand,
One then two become four then eight drops,
The drops turn from little pins to small pebbles
of water,

The grumbling becomes thunder claps,
The pebbles of water hit my skin harder,
My hair sticks to my forehead,
The water clouds my eyes,

Running towards my home,
Closing the door,
Drying my skin,
huddling under the covers for warmth

Beach Nap

Blazing heat, Bright Sun,
Laying in the sand,
Warming up my body,
Sunglasses shielding me from the rays,
Cool drink in one hand,
a book in the other hand,
Breathing in fun,
Breathing out busyness,

Snow flakes

Snow flying in sky,
I see my breath in the air,
Winter has arrived

Ice storm

Close the windows, shut the door,
The wind howls and blows around the house,
The car sits outside on the driveway,
The dark sky crumples and the clouds hide the
light of the moon,
Little taps on the roof, growing closer together,
Now a full wrapping sound on the house,
I look outside and see darkness with hints of
shiny rain drops,
I throw on an extra sweater and curl up on the
couch,

The grey sky wakes me up,
The Trees are heavy with frozen crystals of
water,
One tree branch bends so low with ice that it
touches the ground,
I put on my coat and go outside,
An icy coat cocoons my car,
The sidewalk shines and glistens in the faint
sunlight,
Today is not the day to do work,
Today is the day for hot cocoa and curling up in
front of the fireplace

Hot Chocolate

Pot simmering on the stove,
Hot milk under a slight boil,
Not to hot, not too cold,
Whisking the hard chunks of cocoa into the pot,
The chunks of chocolate from my trip back
home,

Whisk, whisk, whisk,
The white liquid turning brown,
Adding a touch of vanilla, a sprinkle of nutmeg
and the toss of a cinnamon stick,
Turning the pot on low,
Simmering hot chocolate,

Pouring the chocolate into cups,
The steam fogging up the child's glasses,
Turing their nose red,
Warming up their hands from a day in the snow,
A warm hug on a cold day

Grey skies

I breathe in crisp air,
Breath out warmth,
The blue sky and blazing sun warm up my skin,
Red, yellow and brown maple leaves carpet the
front lawn,
Leaving the trees naked and bare,
The sky crumples into a wrinkled piece of paper,
I feel a small pin prick of water,
The wind stirs up the carpet of leaves and takes
them across the street,
The pin pricks of water increase, making my
jacket damp,
I walk into the house, lock the door and look out
the window

Late winter

Puddles of water mark the path,
Patches of green peak through the blankets of
snow,
I change from heavy winter boots to rain boots,
I hang up the heavy puffer jacket and put on the
rain coat,
I breathe in cool air and breath out mild air,
No more hats, no more scarves,
An extra minute of sunlight is added each day,
The snow, ice and frost fall away to reveal the
sun, rain and warmth

Early Spring

The sky opens with the rays of the sun,
Flower buds frame the sky,
The geese pick at the ground, search for food,
I hug myself in the warm air,
Rubbing my arms to warm up to the April air,
I breathe in the warm air of spring,
I breathe out the cold air of winter

Snow Angel

White powder in the field,
Snow flakes softly land on the ground,
The flakes land on my lashes,
I see the six-sided flake on my wool coat,
It disappears as soon as I blink my eyes,

Falling back into the white powder,
I move my hands and legs to create faceless
people in the snow,
I get up and see my angel in the ground,
But falling snowflakes cause my angel to
disappear

A Good ol' Hockey Game

Black puck falls on the ice,
Metal blades chase it,
Carving curves and lines,
As the puck makes its way to the net,

The crowd cheers and yells,
The sun softens the ice,
Heavy breathing in the cold,
The puck continues its trek to the net,

The puck continues to glide on the ice,
Sticks moving it side to side,
The crowd holds its breath,
it hits the side of the net,
moves to the inside of the cage

The crowd erupts in cheers,
The skates stop moving,
The game is over

Cheery Blossoms

Strolling along the winding path,
Small trees with branches that open to the sky,
Branches that hold tiny pink petals,

The sweet scent floating across my nose,
Petals swaying the the soft breeze,
Floating away into the river,

The trees shed their cherry blossoms,
Standing naked without their delicate sweater,
Beauty and innocence falling to the ground

Sugar Ice

Rocket Popsicle,
Sweet Ice Melting in my hand,
Sticky Summertime

Sunrise

Black sky sleeping,
Stars of light fading,
Sun rising in the east,

Sky turning cerulean,
Moonlight fading with the early sun,
The songs of birds waking the earth from sleep,

The sun continues to rise,
Bathing the earth with warmth,
A new day awaits!

Gardening

Scraping the earth,
Poking holes in the ground,
Dropping seeds of potential,

Covering the seeds with dark earth,
Protecting and securing the harvest,
Surrounding the pockets of potential with
vitamins,

Preparing for a bumper crop,
Hope, faith, sunlight and rain are needed,
Let me wait through the summer,
Let me see the what the earth produces from my
hands